Christmas

and other poems

Poems about Christmas as an adult

Andy Higson

Second edition

ISBN: 978-1-7391709-3-6

Dedicated to everyone that I ever spent Christmas Day with or should have.

Wherever you are, Merry Christmas.

Also by Andy Higson

Death by Banality and other poems: A collection of funny, sad, and other poetry

ISBN: 978-1-7391709-5-0

CONTENTS

PART 1 – IT'S CHRISTMAS

PART 2 – THE AFTERMATH

PART 1

-

IT'S CHRISTMAS

Socks for Christmas

One Christmas my stepfather received the sum
total of 21 pairs of socks as presents from all
five family members
It wasn't planned or co-ordinated
Each person independently decided on
Socks and only socks
Imagine unwrapping present after present to
discover
Only socks
And more socks
That last present
Hoping but knowing the inevitable outcome
Feeling that squish of wrapping paper sliding
against fabric
After the last present was opened
Looking down at that pile of socks
And thinking
Do they know me at all?
I am more than a man with feet

The Anti-Santa

She goes around children's bedrooms
Stealing toys
She's in your living room
Regurgitating mince pies
Tunnelling underground from home to home
Powered by... I can't think what the opposite of a reindeer would be
Maybe some spider or an octopus with shovels for arms
Not a soul can sleep because they are terrified
You hear a noise in the middle of an unbearably sweaty July night
You run downstairs
There's a no-bearded lady stealing things from your front room
"No! No! No!" she shouts as she puts them in her sack
Or possibly; "Oh! Oh! Oh!"
But she's definitely not jolly
Every Christmas she tries to shoot down Father Christmas' sleigh with an array of increasingly sophisticated weaponry

Anti-Santa is not to be confused with Aunty Santa
That's a completely different person
And poem

The last few hours of Christmas Day

Everyone's asleep but me
It's all done but for the doing
Which means it isn't done yet
It's the last few hours of Christmas Day

I think about my life
All the Christmases I can remember
And the Christmases to come
One less now

I think about all the people that I’ve ever spent
Christmas Day with
That I don't know any more

Midnight comes and goes
Life goes on
For now

Too soon

I'd gone for a run
It was towards the end of August
The day was every kind of hot
The heat made it hurt to run but it made me feel alive
Heightened by the remote possibility that I could collapse and die
I thought about the cold shower that awaited me
I went in to the supermarket for a bottle of water
The five-pound note I always tucked in my sock finally paid off

Wait

There was a display of mince pies as you walked in
But it was summer
Christmas and all that entailed had not been conceived of yet
I looked at this monstrous absurdity
It was so wrong
I felt ill
Oh no
I was going to be sick
I put my hands in front of my mouth

Which merely ensured I had sick-covered hands
I looked up at the horrified strangers
All a witness to my shame
I panicked and ran out
Wailing “I’m sorry” over my shoulder through my sick-covered hands
I never went to that supermarket again
And I would need a new running route

Not today

It is snowing
The wind is blowing
I am going
Back to bed

It is too cold
I am too old
Let it be told
I am staying in bed

It is very dark
The choice is stark
Go to the park
Or lie in bed

Outside is wet
But do not fret
Continue this duet
And stay with me in bed

Waiting for Santa

As a kid on Christmas Eve
I tried to stay awake all night so I could see
Father Christmas
In our family tradition
Father Christmas would leave our presents
beneath the Christmas tree
And a stocking at the end of our bed
With little toys and sweets and always a single
tangerine
With every bump and creak I thought
Maybe this is him

One year
I heard Father Christmas open that door
I kept my eyes shut and didn't open them until
he left
It's only when they are about to be realised that
we find out if we want our dreams to come true

The Christmas Fun Squad

You can see it in their eyes
Pure
Fucking
Insanity
Barely caged, controlled throughout the year
A maniac that is only kept in check
By a prison made of their own dullness
And lack of imagination
But come Christmas
They can no longer control themselves
Panting, gagging, salivating
As the 1st December approaches
They barely make it
Before they fucking explode
All over the rest of us

Christmas is safe fun
There's a clear, strict laid-out structure
It's fun but not too much fun
Not fun that could go anywhere
It's fun for dullards
Dull-fun
Worked out over successive Christmases
Every nook smoothed
Every cranny filled-in
It's time-limited and more importantly
They don't have to think

Socks for Christmas

It’s organised fun
And they get to do the organising

The kind of people who when fascism arrives
Say “I don’t really do politics
I’m just doing my job”

That escalated I know

Wrap this

I should go on a course
To learn how to wrap presents
So that they are perfect
Beautiful, pristine little boxes of Christmas magic
Just like in the books and films and other people's lives
But I don't
Because even some truly magical ideas
May be worth thinking fondly on
But are not worth getting out of bed for

The best Christmas

I was 8 years old
Every Christmas Day we'd walk to my grandparents around 11am
Across Bolton from Daubhill to Great Lever
At times it seemed we were the only people around
The backstreets in that part of Bolton were covered in packed-down snow
There wasn't a lot of it
But there was enough
We walked down one backstreet, near a looming and blackened Victorian primary school, and kept falling over
We all started laughing and couldn't stop
There wasn't always a lot of laughter
But there was that day
We eventually made it to my grandparents and spent Christmas Day together
It was a good Christmas
The Christmas that I judge every other Christmas against

The worst Christmas

...maybe I shouldn't put every sad thing about
me on paper and show it to the world
There's enough sadness out there

Grandad Christmas

I miss my grandad
I miss the Christmases that I never spent with him
I was a teenager and life was too hard
Inexplicably hard
I couldn't leave the house
So I spent it alone
A part of me
Always will be

Almost Father Christmas

It nearly happened this year
But I'm not quite ready
Not quite ripe
I'm getting there though
My belly is getting bigger
My beard is getting whiter
One Christmas soon
Someone will ask if I'm free to help out...
Or perhaps I'll need the money

I'll be a Father Christmas
Suit
Beard
Boots
Sack
The whole shabang
I'll enjoy it too
The kids with a wonder and laughter that is now incomprehensibly joyous to an ever more old and broken man
But behind every Father Christmas is a little boy
Who no longer believes
Is that beautiful or something else?
Is it the knowledge that the laughter ends

Rap that

Christmas was going on forever
And not in a good or magical way
In particular
Christmas songs were being played in the office
Loudly
Perhaps too loudly
Perhaps more loudly than was reasonable for a workplace with still several weeks to go until Christmas Day
A couple of us decided to throw some Christmas rap songs onto the laptop where the office music playlist lived
We were just two little boys who wanted some fat funky beats for Christmas
We were also bored and were tantalised by the prospect of Christmas chaos
The Office Christmas Fun Squad slammed it down
They frantically waddled over
As hard and fast as they could go
They were furious
We had done something and they could not understand why
They were angry at us and angry at themselves and so even more angry at us
We had ruined Christmas

Socks for Christmas

Good
Not all versions of Christmas have equal merit

Sprouts

The first time I heard about baking sprouts
Wow, I thought
Baking sprouts
As opposed to boiling them

Of course
How had it never occurred to me
I've not boiled anything since

Baking sprouts
It was my way out of bland sprouts and bland food
The way out of boiling
Or rather the way spr-out

Christmas drinkers

Around the first week of December
When the very first office Christmas meals and parties occur
You see the first one
Something isn't quite right in the first few seconds as the first zombie
Contemplates their new world
They look normal
But...
They’re different
The rhythm is not right
They jerk and jolt
Hello Christmas drinker

The kind of person who only really gets drunk at Christmas
They’re not used to it
They're not pros
They haven’t put the training and hard work in all year around
They think anyone can do it
That it’s easy

And it's 7pm outside Clapham train station
They shuffle off home
I hope they make it

Pub etiquette

There's at least 10 of them
Not a round to be found
Each buys their own drink
One by one by one by...
He doesn't realise it's his turn
She needs a few seconds to catch up
He adds a couple of lines to whatever bullshit conversation they're having
Before turning to the bartender
Only then do they carefully consider their options
"What do I feel like... today?" they announce to the world
Everyone else waits for them
As they stand there...
And I don't mean to be unfestive, but...
Each and every one of them an oblivious, clueless arsehole

When the bombs fall
When the earth is ablaze
It won't be all bad

Father Father Christmas

Imagine if your dad was Father Christmas
It would complicate things
Writing a letter asking for what you want
Being put on the naughty list

Dad would sleep in all Christmas Day but
You'd get to hang around with all the elves

It would make for some great arguments as you grew older
"Hey Dad, trying giving a shit about me instead of all these kids you're not the dad of!"

Would you know other kids? What would they say to you?
“Your dad isn’t real. He doesn’t exist!”

Just take the day off

I read about a woman who walked 12 miles through the snow
To get to work
For some job in an office or a shop
Not a job where people would die or face great hardship if someone didn't show up
They weren't a doctor or even someone who just a whole bunch of other people depended on
"Isn't that amazing?" everyone said
No
Actually
It's the opposite of amazing
It's unamazing
Give me a story about the woman who didn't walk 12 miles through the snow
On waking she realised the futility of trying to get to work
The recklessness of endangering herself and would-be rescuers
So she went back to bed
Thinking
Fuck that

Sometimes you just have to take the day off
Enjoy yourself as best you can
And start again tomorrow

Or even the day after that

Father Christmas vs. Santa

Brits say Father Christmas
Americans say Santa

But that's not quite true
In Britain we use both

I don't care that much
But I care a little

I used to insist on Father Christmas
Then I chilled out
There are more important things going on
My kids use the terms interchangeably
And the last of my will to even think about it evaporates

Santa's fine but a little too informal
For the name of a winter god with a dark past
Santa's fun but he smacks of being a capitalist stooge
Some people don't mind that
I do
Just a little

Wishing for snow

Every day from October to March
I wished for snow when I was a little boy
To wake up
Pull back the curtains
And to see snow
Like in one of those Christmas cards

It so rarely came

One day, much older, I realised
People die when it snows
People die every day
But more people die when it snows
Because they were homeless
Or couldn't afford to put the heating on
Because they were too poor or too old
Or both

Even knowing then what I know now
I still think that I may have wished for snow
The wishing didn't cause the snow

I could have wished for the snow and to live in a country where that didn't mean people would die
But wishes don't come true

It feels wrong to wish for people not to die from the cold
It's not something to wish for
Wishing isn't needed
Nor magic or divine intervention
We could change it all overnight
If we wanted to
Collectively
We just don't want it enough
To vote for decency
And not believe lies about why it's okay for people to die
Because it gets cold

We can't make it snow
No matter how hard we try
It just happens
Or it doesn't

We could stop people from dying because it gets cold
But we don't

Christmas Songs

They stop playing Christmas songs on the radio at midnight
Not at 1 or 2 or 3 am but midnight
On the dot
00:00
That's it
That's the Christmas cutoff
I can't move on from this
It makes little sense
In March and October, they don't move the clocks forward or backward at midnight
They wait until 1 or 2am
Until more people are asleep
It just works better that way
Maybe they think about people writing in
Complaining
Not everyone should be listened to

Imagine driving back
Through the snow
The kids asleep in the back
The radio's on
And at midnight the Christmas songs stop
No
It's not right
I'm not saying go on forever
But Christmas Day gets to finish a little late

It gets to take its time
2am maybe 3am
It is Christmas after all

Christmas as an adult

I'm a man
I am
So I have the burden and honour of carrying the Christmas tree home

Reaching deep inside
I don't shout at the people who decide
That I should be the one to move aside on the pavement though I am carrying a Christmas tree
And they are not

I stop
Put down the Christmas tree and stare at them
As they stare at me
And wonder if this time there'll be a fight
Will I punch them in the throat?

"I guess Boxing Day came early" I say to them as they lie on the floor
Before I continue on home
The Christmas tree weighs nothing
I have never been more alive

Father Christmas vs. Death

If Father Christmas exists
So must Death
(The anthropomorphic version)
Do they ever meet?
Rather awkwardly in a living room on
Christmas or maybe socially
Does Death have dominion over Father
Christmas?
When the last human dies
Death will be there and not just for that last
human
The Easter Bunny, Jack Frost
They're all for it
Could Father Christmas and Death have a fight
Could Father Christmas kill death?
What a Christmas present
The end of Death
And death
From Father Christmas
Would we ever forgive him?

Perhaps it is time to go to bed

The First Christmas

Imagine the first Christmas
Not the first, first Christmas
But the first one where it was first celebrated
Why has Dad brought a tree into the living room?
He must be pissed
I heard that!
I'm a visionary
I'm the future
Get that fucking tree out of this house
No! It's staying
It's magical
It's got a squirrel in it!

A poem about Jesus

I want to write at least one poem about Jesus
In a book of Christmas poems
But it's hard to write poems about Jesus
Much less funny ones
So this will have to do

Christmas Eve Shopper

I used to go out on Christmas Eve
Around midday
To the pound shop
6 presents for £6
I was done within 10 minutes
I would celebrate with a hot cheese pasty

I never understood why people got so stressed out about Christmas
Go to the pound shop the day before Christmas Eve if you are that worried

Alternative views of the Nativity

If I was one of those animals who no longer
had the stable to myself
I would be furious
Who are these people
Why are there wise men here?
What's a wise man?
Is that an angel?
I have a hard day of doing whatever animals
have to do tomorrow
I don't get Christmas Day off
No one does yet

How many hotels or inns did downtown
Bethlehem in the year AD 1 have?

Couldn't an angel have made a room booking?
They told some shepherds
Why not tell the guy running the Bed &
Breakfast by apparition or just a polite inquiry

It is a wild system of government that both
makes everyone return to their place of birth
for a census and allows an order to murder all
children under the age of 2
I'm not voting for those guys
Some people would

How can I still not really know what
frankincense or myrrh are?

Do the elves have a trade union?

Are Santa's elves in a trade union?
They don't need a union some of you say
Santa treats them well
If they don't like it
They should get a job elsewhere
Why are people like me constantly trying to stir things up?

What do you know about their working conditions?
Not a thing!
Does it anger you that I ask these questions
That elves have hopes and dreams
Good
You're the enemy of all mankind
And elfkind

Christmas News

Not a lot happens over Christmas
In terms of the news
But people still die
Famous and not
Like any other day
Maybe more
The news is full of such stories
Because
There's nothing else to talk about
And not that many people watch the news over Christmas

Christmas Dead

Imagine dying on Christmas Day
You overcome the excitement of Christmas Eve
and finally manage to get to sleep
Then you die
Forever waiting for Christmas morning
Or during the presents being opened
During the meal
At night

There may be no good way to die
But there's definitely no good way to die on
Christmas Day
Any other day would be better
Jesus left it until Easter
Didn't want to leave a bad feeling vibe over
Christmas

Every year when you were a kid
Desperate for Christmas
Just hastening the anniversary of your doom

People shouldn't die at Christmas
But they do anyway

Even if you could somehow pause it all and
stop people dying over the Christmas holidays
Imagine that first day back at work

Christmas Tat

I used to love buying absolute tat at Christmas
The inanity of it all
The indecent consumerism
Maybe it was a defence mechanism

One Christmas I was playing with a finger
puppet that was a bear dressed as an elf
I realised
Instead of giving my children a better world
With one piece of tat at a time
I was helping burn it down

The worst Christmas present ever

Christmas Every Day

There's a house in Norwich
The outside walls are covered in Christmas lights
All year long
They sit
Wait
Dormant
Almost all year long

I used to think that was insane
I understand it a bit more
Now I'm older
Having embraced my laziness
And caring a lot less about what other people think
I can imagine the first couple of Christmases taking it all down
But one year, I'd think
Why not just leave it all up

Or perhaps now I'm just sufficiently insane

Imagine switching on those lights
After 10 months

It would feel like cumming

Party on a Thursday

They always held the office party on a Thursday
Was it that no-one was willing to give up their
Friday or Saturday
Or that the venues were slightly cheaper
Both

The Friday was horrendous
Getting for work by 9am
It was the one day you couldn't ring in sick
Because everyone
Would know

But one year
A guy rang in and said he had food poisoning
from the fish the night before
His manager was so angry that he cried
Others nodded in sympathy

That's what happens when you have a party on
a Thursday

Christmas Pudding

Are Christmas puddings good?
Not morally
As in - are they tasty?

Every year I think about it
I've still not got an answer
Christmas puddings aren't unpleasant but
people don't eat it all year around...

The true test of any seasonal food
Is whether it is eaten outside the season
A-seasonally
No one eats pumpkin pie in March
It's disgusting
If it was really tasty you'd have it every other
week
Chocolate doesn't need a seasonal holiday to
get eaten

At least you can set a Christmas pudding on
fire
That's no small thing
Only Christmas can get away with setting food
on fire
Try that shit at Easter
You'd be put away

I wish you a Merry Christmas

"I wish you a Merry Christmas..."
Do you
Do you really

I don't think you do
I detect, at best, a distinct indifference to the plight and well-being of your fellow man

It is said so often it's like a snowflake in the wind
But you should say it
It is good for the soul to wish a stranger happiness and to mean it
For though it may do no good at all for them
It will do good for you

Not that that is why you should do it

Die Hard is a Christmas film

Some people think it is
Some people think... otherwise
But the point is
What kind of person do you want to be?

You can't be the kind of person who has never thought about it
It's too late for you

You don't want to be the kind of person who doesn't care about it or think it doesn't matter
You know it does

So you have to make a choice

Do you want to be Mr. Fucking Twee – Grand Guardian of all things shit and awful?
Chuckleheading your way around December as part of the Christmas Fun Squad?
Of course not
You'd rather die

You want just one little present in Santa's big sack where it's 1988 and Bruce Willis is fucking up terrorists on Christmas Eve and Alan Rickman is acting the shit out of it

Socks for Christmas

It's Christmas Eve
John McClane has lost his way, but he'll find it again
He's lost his family, but they will be reunited
Nothing can stop a family's happiness at Christmas...
...Except for the family itself

Christmas doesn't have to suck all the time
You don't have to suck all the time

Christmas can be rad and awesome with cool motherfuckers
Not all the time
Apparently
But Christmas is for everyone
Not just jerks who think Die Hard isn't a Christmas film

PART 2

-

THE AFTERMATH

Boxing Day

You don't think about Boxing Day until it's here
It's always the afterthought
There's no countdown to Boxing Day
Its existence is entirely dependent on its far
bigger, more famous, more loved sibling
Like the morning after a party
Inevitable but not part of the anticipation or
the planning

We still don't really know what it's for
No one's boxing anything

All the Americans reading this thinking
So what the fuck is Boxing Day?
No one knows
No one

George Washington on the first Christmas Day
after independence
Banned it
"I don't know what it's for!
It's maddening!
We're done with it!"
And that was that

January 25th

It's like it never happened
One month to the day
Was it all a dream?
A Christmas dream
No

There are little clues
A mass of pine needles on the pavement
Like the outline of a dead body at a crime scene
After the body's been taken to the morgue
Or the very last seasonally-themed items in the supermarket
Reduced and waiting

You still see some of those pine needles as late as March
Like the evidence of a crime
Before a wind finally sweeps last Christmas away

They hunt foxes on Boxing Day

Like most normal people
I don't think about the people that go hunting on Boxing Day
Until I see them on the news that very day
All dressed up to kill

It's illegal to kill the foxes now
To hunt them down with dogs
Until they are too tired
And are ripped apart

Imagine spending Christmas Day hoping that tomorrow
Some dogs will accidentally kill a fox
And that you will get to see it

I would put you at the very top of the naughty list

It is my Christmas tree

Some neighbours deposit their spent Christmas trees on the pavement
Where they are eventually collected and disposed of by the local authorities

That's the easy way
Of which
I do not choose to partake

Instead
I leave it in the garden for several months
Undercover where it slowly dries out
Then one completely random day
Anytime from March to August
Using a combination of pliers, a saw, and a hedge trimmer
I remove all the branches until there is just a trunk
Which I place somewhere in the garden
The branches go in the compost
The garden is slowly filling up with tree trunks

It's become a tradition
Now I've started
I don't dare stop

April 4th

It's April 4th
I'm trying to think of poems about Christmas
But spring has arrived and the sun is shining
Christmas can wait

It's June and I'm currently sweating my balls off
How many poems can I write about Christmas
Enough for the very smallest of small books?
We'll see

I try and think about Christmas
What is Christmas?
I've never been less sure
This is poem number 39
1,371 words in
I take off my shorts and sit at the desk in my underwear
I decide to eat ice cream for dinner

September 12th

100 days until Christmas
I tell people
They don’t know what to say
There's nothing for them to say

Because I’m not actually saying anything

When do you take the decorations down?

Some people take their decorations down early
Because someone they love died shortly after
Christmas
How very sad and beautiful

Others take them down early
Because they can't stand sitting around and
just enjoy being alive
They can't sit around
And just be

Those of us who keep them up to the bitter end
We're in a hut
Beset by snow and storms
We keep those decorations up
They are a light in winter
Against the dark
The dark will always come but
There's no hurry

Calendar

Idiots everywhere:
It's that crazy time of year between Christmas and New Year
What day is it!?!?
Does anyone know?!?!

I don't know what day it is!
(It's the 28th December)

I don't know what day it is!!
(It's the 29th December)

I don't know what day it is!!!
(It's the 30th December)

Every year

They don't deserve this time off

New Year's Eve

For years I didn't enjoy New Year's Eve
The expectation is unreal
Positively inhuman

If you're single there's a pressure about finding
the love of your life to kiss at midnight
That seems unfair to people who have not
kissed anyone all year long

Some willingly spend hours surrounded by tens
of thousands of other people in the centre of a
city

At least a few of these people will be annoying
How long is it going to take to get home
Is anyone else thinking about this?

Counting down from 10 to 1 is rarely fun
Standing around other people is rarely fun
Other people are rarely fun

I had one good New Year's Eve
On a rooftop
I watched the reflection of the fireworks on a
building
And I held someone close

Last year
I played a boardgame and was asleep by midnight
Sometimes
There isn't always a way to win
And
The only way to not lose is by not playing

New Year's Day

From midnight on New Year's Eve/Day
You can be back at work
31 hours later
The alarm goes off 28 hours later
Minus 16 hours of sleep
That's 12 hours of the holidays left
Tick tick
Tick tick

Back at work

It almost falls apart
That first day back at work
Society, civilization
All of it
Waking up
Thinking 36 hours ago it was New Year's Eve
And you were having fun
Or wishing you were
Enjoying your new life of not being at work
That part of you that thought this would go on forever
Now you're at a bus stop
Or stuck in traffic
With every other fuck-up
No one says a thing
United and divided by our shame
What system is this?
You get to work and wait for the day to end
Wait for the weekend, for your next holiday
Wait for next Christmas
Do anything but live here and now

Christmas Tree Massacre

You see the first one around the 28th
Every year it's somehow a surprise
An ex-Christmas tree is just lying there on the pavement
Unadorned and spent
Bereft of purpose

Just one
Then two
Then more
Then all
Until there's a mound of them
Like a Christmas tree of Christmas trees
Waiting to go wherever former-Christmas trees go

Christmas isn’t dying
It’s already dead
This is the aftermath
The funeral and the wake

A long, hard Christmas

It had been a long, hard Christmas
Several of the last few days were strong competitors for the title of the single most awful day of my life

It was closer to New Year's Eve than Christmas
I met an old friend at the pub in Victoria Station in Manchester
It was open and we were both travelling by train from opposite directions
I would occasionally glance at the giant Christmas tree in the corner of the station
It looked absurd
Even mocking
Christmas was a spell and the magic had gone
Christmas had never seemed so much of a lie
Still
I took some solace in my conviction that I would not take my own life during time off work
That is what January is for

...

Things got better
Nothing magic truly disappears

Blue Monday

The most depressing day of the year is the third Monday in January

It has been scientifically calculated by marketing people to help promote recruitment agencies

Who could doubt those two titans of human civilisation?

...

The first Monday in January has at least the novelty of being the first Monday

There's an energy to the awfulness

The second Monday is hard...

...but it's the third Monday that it really hits you

This is your life

Time to be depressed

...

Christmas withdrawal is at its peak

Not just the big day nor the week or two around it but the weeks of looking forward to it

The distraction of it all kept away the cold, wet, darkness

That darkness is still there

It always was

Did I mention how cold and wet the darkness is?

That's the worst kind of darkness

Or coldness

Or wetness

...

Now it's the third Monday in January

And it's only the 17th of January

Spring is three months away

And you don't just have no money

You have minus money

You are paying the system for this life of yours

If you're not depressed

Why aren't you?

...

I love Blue Monday

I stride into the office and announce

"TODAY IS THE MOST DEPRESSING DAY OF THE YEAR"

I get to talk about depression all day long

Not just about being depressed (though that too) but my thoughts about depression and the flaws of modern life

...

Just remember

Anyone can get depressed in January

Try getting depressed in July

Next Christmas

25th July
We are closer to next Christmas
Then we are to the last one

Yet
Everyone's walking around
Enjoying the sunshine
Pretending that they don't know
Pretending that they are thinking of other things

A few words from the author

I hope you enjoyed *Socks for Christmas*.

I added 'Poems about Christmas as an adult' as the subtitle so adults knew what they were in for and to help reduce the possibility of any children accidentally receiving this as a gift.

- Father Christmas versus Santa

In the UK people use the term Father Christmas whereas in the US people say Santa. I have used both terms, sometimes interchangeably, sometimes not. I used whichever term felt right.

I could say a lot more about this. But I won't.

If you're not from the UK or the US, let me know if you use a different name. I'll try and put it in the sequel.

- Boxing Day

To people in countries that don't have a Boxing Day. I don't know what Boxing Day is. No-one does. But it exists.

I realise you will know no more than was the case before you started reading this. However, sometimes you just have to acknowledge things and then we can all move on.

I am sorry there weren't more poems about Jesus and the nativity etc... it's just really hard to write something funny about such things. It's far easier to write something about, say sprouts. And I only managed one poem about sprouts.

I wish you the very merriest of Christmases and the happiest New Year.

Andy Higson

Printed in Great Britain
by Amazon

50304887R00047